364 DAYS OF
THANKSGIVING

ANDREW C. SCHROER

NORTHWESTERN PUBLISHING HOUSE
Milwaukee, Wisconsin

TO MY WIFE, CLARIZA; MY DAUGHTER, ISABEL; AND MY SON, ANDY.
AFTER JESUS, THEY ARE WHAT I AM MOST THANKFUL FOR.

Second printing, 2016

Cover photos: Shutterstock
Art Director: Karen Knutson
Design Team: Carianne Ciriacks, Sarah Messner

Northwestern Publishing House
1250 N. 113th St., Milwaukee, WI 53226-3284
www.nph.net
© 2015 Northwestern Publishing House
Published 2015
Printed in the United States of America
ISBN 978-0-8100-2675-9
ISBN 978-0-8100-2676-6 (e-book)

TABLE OF CONTENTS

WHY WRITE A BOOK
ABOUT BEING THANKFUL?

A few years ago, a young mother tried to commit suicide. By God's grace she was unsuccessful. Because of a connection her family had with our church, her husband called me the next morning, asking me to visit her in the hospital.

As I spoke with her, it became obvious that she was deeply depressed about her marriage and family. The doctors ordered that she receive medication and professional counseling. She also asked that I visit her once a week.

Feeling overwhelmed by the situation, I asked a psychologist friend for help. He explained to me that depression is often anger turned inward. He suggested that she was so angry about the problems in her life, she couldn't see the good God had given her. Among other things, he advised me to have her keep a notebook by her bed.

Every morning and every evening, the young mother was to write down one good thing in her life—but each time it had to be something different. She couldn't repeat the same blessing even once.

Over the next few weeks, as her list grew longer, her attitude grew brighter. She began to notice all the blessings God had given her, especially God's greatest gift of forgiveness. She began to see that even the problems were part of God's gracious plan for her life. She began to smile again. Soon she was weaned off the antidepressant medication.

That young mother was the inspiration for this book.

Are you depressed? Are you frustrated by the problems and struggles in your life? The secret to happiness isn't to rid your life of problems. The secret to happiness isn't getting what you want. The secret to happiness is recognizing what you have in Christ.

This book is about seeing what God has done for you.

I am personally grateful to those who have helped make this book possible. I especially would like to thank Pastor Michael and Rachel Hartman; Christy Bagasao, owner and editor of *The Simple Homemaker* blog; and Julie Wietzke, editor of *Forward in Christ* magazine, for their valuable insights and encouragement.

But most of all, I thank my God and Savior, Jesus Christ. Everything I am and everything I have is because of him.

CHAPTER 1
OVERWHELMING GRATITUDE

---

*"Gratitude is not only the greatest of virtues,
but the parent of all others."* — CICERO

*"A thankful heart hath a
continual feast."* — W.J. CAMERON

The British author Charles Dickens once commented that we are somewhat backward here in America. Instead of having just one Thanksgiving Day each year, we should have 364. "Use that one day just for complaining and griping," he said. "Use the other 364 days to thank God each day for the many blessings he has showered upon you."

That is the simple premise of this little book. At the end of this book is a journal. My hope and prayer is that over the next 364 days, you take the time to think about and write down one thing each day for which you are thankful. There is a catch, though. It has to be a different blessing each day. Throughout the entire year you cannot repeat the same blessing even once.

On day 365, instead of spending the day griping and complaining as Charles Dickens recommends, read through your entire *364 Days of Thanksgiving Journal*. My prayer is that through this simple exercise, God will help you grow in your love and appreciation for his many and varied gifts.

Before we begin our yearlong journey of thanks, however, let's remind ourselves what it means to be thankful, what it means to be *overwhelmingly* thankful, and how we display that thankfulness in our lives.

AN EXAMPLE OF OVERWHELMING GRATITUDE

Jesus once was walking on the road to Jerusalem. As he approached a small village, he suddenly heard what sounded like whispers in the wind. He glanced around. There, standing about a football field away, were ten emaciated, disfigured men. Their voices were strained and weak, but they gathered the strength to get Jesus' attention.

"Jesus, Master, have pity on us!" they cried.

They were lepers. Leprosy, also known as Hansen's disease, has been all but eradicated from our world today. In Jesus' day, however, leprosy was a plague. There were no treatments. A leper's march toward death was long and painful. Due to the contagious nature of the disease and the stigma attached to it, most lepers were sent away from society to live in enclaves called leper colonies.

In ancient Israel, lepers were considered "unclean." People suffering from such diseases were forbidden to join in the worship at the temple or to live with the rest of God's people. If someone were to approach them, they were to cry out, "Unclean! Stay away!"

So these men stood at a distance. They didn't come near Jesus. They simply called to him in their weak and scratchy voices, "Jesus, Master, have pity on us!"

YOU CAN'T BE THANKFUL WITHOUT HAVING SOMEONE TO THANK.

When Jesus heard their faint cries for help and saw their sore-filled faces, he did have pity on them. He yelled to them, "Go, show yourselves to the priests."

If people were to recover from leprosy, they would need to show themselves to a priest. The priest would declare them "clean" and able to rejoin society. Until the priest declared them clean, they were still outcasts.

The men did what Jesus said. They turned and set off to see the priests. As they did, their pain dissipated. Their sores disappeared. Their voices returned. Nine of the ten picked up the pace. They happily hurried to see the priests so they could return to their homes and lives. But one stopped. When he realized he was healed, he ran back to Jesus as fast as he could, praising God in a loud voice. He threw himself at Jesus' feet and thanked him. Luke tells us he was a Samaritan, a foreigner.

When we hear that story, we often find ourselves angry with the other nine men. How could they be so ungrateful?

If you read the story of the ten lepers in Luke chapter 17, though, you will notice that it does not say the other nine were not thankful. In fact, they did exactly what Jesus told them to do. They went to show themselves to the priests. We can only imagine that when they were given a clean bill of health, they thanked and praised God as they returned to their families and lives.

The point of the story is not that the other nine were ungrateful. The point is how *overwhelmingly* grateful the Samaritan was. He put off the one thing that he had desired for so long—to be told by the priest he could go home—and put off being reunited with his family and friends to first return and thank the person who had healed him.

The Samaritan understood that thankfulness is not some nebulous, vague feeling. Gratitude cannot exist where there is no giver. You can't be thankful without having someone to thank.

The Samaritan realized it was God who deserved the credit. He recognized it was Jesus who healed him. So he ran. He cried. He fell at Jesus' feet and thanked him with overwhelming gratitude.

AN EXAMPLE OF OVERWHELMING GENEROSITY

Not too long after his encounter with the ten lepers, Jesus visited the city of Jericho. In just a few short days, on Palm Sunday, he would enter Jerusalem surrounded by adoring fans. Even now, crowds gathered around him. The paparazzi hounded him. The frenzied crowds reached out to touch him.

A man named Zacchaeus was part of that crowd in Jericho, but Zacchaeus had a problem. He was short. He couldn't see over the crowd.

OVERWHELMING GRATITUDE LEADS TO OVERWHELMING GENEROSITY.

Zacchaeus wanted to see Jesus, however, so he climbed a sycamore-fig tree just to catch a glimpse of him. When Jesus reached the tree, he looked straight up into the limbs and said, "Zacchaeus, come down immediately. I must stay at your house today."

A gasp went out from the crowd. They knew who Zacchaeus was. Zacchaeus was a tax collector. In our day, someone who collects taxes isn't always very popular. In Zacchaeus' day, tax collectors were considered the scum of society.

You see, the Roman government hired individuals from each country to collect the imperial taxes. These tax collectors were required to collect a certain amount from each individual. If a tax collector could get more from each person during his collection, he could keep the difference. Oh, and behind the tax collector stood Roman soldiers, making sure the people paid.

Suffice it to say, tax collectors became very rich. They were considered corrupt politicians, traitors to their fellow people, the scum of society.

Now Jesus was going to stay at Zacchaeus' house. The people began to whisper. Jesus' enemies began to mutter, "Doesn't he know that he is going to be the guest of a 'sinner'?"

Zacchaeus, however, was overwhelmingly excited to have such a famous guest come to his house. Luke chapter 19 doesn't tell us what the two discussed in Zacchaeus' home, but we can be sure that Jesus spoke about sin and forgiveness. That was the most important message people needed to hear.

Realizing his sin and meeting his Savior changed Zacchaeus. He was so overwhelmingly thankful, he stood up and said, "Look, Lord! Here and now I give half of my possessions to the poor, and if I have cheated anybody out of anything, I will pay back four times the amount." Overwhelming gratitude is more than words. Overwhelming gratitude leads to overwhelming generosity.

Are you thankful? I'm assuming you are. You recognize God's goodness and many of the blessings he has showered upon you. You say "thank you" to God in your prayers. You tell people that you are blessed. You are thankful.

My prayer is that this book helps you become *overwhelmingly* thankful. My prayer is that you find the joy of being overwhelmingly generous.

CHAPTER 2
THE SECRET TO BEING OVERWHELMINGLY GRATEFUL

"The unthankful heart . . . discovers no mercies;
but let the thankful heart sweep through the
day and, as the magnet finds the iron, so it will
find, in every hour, some heavenly blessings!"
— HENRY WARD BEECHER

I am wary of any book or chapter of a book that begins with the words "The Secret to. . . . " Our world today is always looking for a quick fix, a silver bullet, an easy solution to all its problems. We would love to know the secret to six-pack abs or financial security.

This chapter is not a silver bullet. It's not a pill that will make your body fat melt away or all your problems disappear. There is no secret to being overwhelmingly grateful. I'm not about to reveal a great and profound mystery. The secret to being overwhelmingly grateful is simply to open your eyes.

THE SECRET TO BEING OVERWHELMINGLY GRATEFUL IS TO RECOGNIZE WHAT YOU HAVE.

Everything was new. The earth still had that new car smell. God had just finished his wondrous work of creation. Color and life were everywhere. Dinosaurs roamed the earth. Animals lived in perfect harmony with one another. The air was fresh and clean. It was paradise.

The Lord God formed the man from the dust of the ground and breathed into his nostrils the breath of life. He placed man in that perfect paradise and said to him, "This is my gift to you." But something was missing.

God said, "It is not good for the man to be alone" (Genesis 2:18). Man wasn't complete, so God decided to create for him a helper, a companion.

AS SINFUL HUMAN BEINGS, WE TEND TO TAKE GOD'S BLESSINGS FOR GRANTED.

Before he did, however, God had all the animals come to Adam. He told Adam to give them names. The dogs he called dogs. The cats he called cats. The platypuses he called platypuses.

Have you ever wondered why God did that? He was about to make a companion for Adam, but first he had the man name all the animals. Why would he do that?

The book of Genesis tells us that when Adam was done naming the animals, he came to a realization. All the dogs had other dogs. All the cats had other cats. All the platypuses had other platypuses. But for Adam, no suitable companion was found.

That's when God caused Adam to fall into a deep sleep. He took one of Adam's ribs and from it formed the woman.

When Adam woke up, he was overwhelmed with appreciation for this companion God had given him. That is when Adam composed the first love poem: "This is now bone of my bones and flesh of my flesh; she shall be called 'woman,' for she was taken out of man" (Genesis 2:23).

It doesn't sound very romantic, does it? But think about it. Adam was saying, "She is a part of me. She completes me."

Adam was overwhelmingly grateful for Eve, in part because God had first let him see that he was missing something. Have you ever noticed how much more we appreciate things when we have to live without them for a while?

As sinful human beings, we tend to take God's blessings for granted. We often don't notice the amazing gift of air conditioning until it breaks down in the middle of summer. We aren't aware of how much we depend on electricity until the power goes out and we stare at one another, wondering what to do without our TVs, cell phones, and computers.

A wise, old pastor once told me, "The secret to happiness is not getting what you want; it's wanting what you've got." We spend so much time focusing on what we don't have, on what other people have, on what we want to have, that we lose sight of what we do have.

The secret to being overwhelmingly grateful is to recognize what you have.

That is the simple premise of this book. By writing down a different blessing each day for which you are thankful, you will recognize what you have.

THERE IS NO SUCH THING AS A POOR CHRISTIAN.

And we have so much. One of the biggest obstacles to overwhelming gratitude is the overwhelming wealth of our country. We see our neighbor's big house and fancy car. We see movie stars and million-dollar athletes living extravagant lives. We begin to think we are poor, or at least that we aren't rich.

According to the online calculator entitled *Global Rich List*, if your household earned more than $52,000 in the year 2012, you are richer than 97 percent of the world. That means nearly seven billion people in the world are poorer than you. If you earn just half that, $26,000, you are still richer than 90 percent of the world. Even the poorest Americans are among the richest people in the world.

Look at what we have. We have homes with air conditioning and central heating. We have comfortable beds and flat screen TVs. In fact, many of us have more TVs in our homes than we have people.

Because we have so much stuff, one of our biggest problems is finding where to put it all. We complain because our closets are too small. We buy bigger refrigerators. We spend hundreds of dollars a year to rent storage space.

Even if God doesn't give you all those material possessions, you are still rich because you have a home waiting for you in the mansions of heaven, where the streets are paved with gold. You are rich because your Savior, Jesus, became poor for you.

Two thousand years ago, the all-powerful King of the universe left behind the riches and glory of heaven to be born in a manure-smelling barn. He left behind the glory, the comfort, the perfection of heaven to become one of us. He came to be our substitute, to suffer and to die in our place. On the cross, God himself suffered the punishment we deserve for all our ingratitude and selfishness, for all our worry and doubt, for every bad thing we have ever done.

Because he did, we are forgiven. God is not going to punish you because he punished Jesus in your place. Whoever believes in Jesus will be saved. That is God's promise, and God doesn't lie. You are forgiven. You have heaven. Therefore, you are rich.

Even if you were living in the rubble of war-torn Afghanistan or sleeping on a dirt floor in a straw hut in Africa, you would still be rich because you have heaven. There is no such thing as a poor Christian.

Did you get that? Because that's important. There is no such thing as a poor Christian. You are not, nor will you ever be, poor. You are a son or daughter of the King of the universe. You are forgiven and loved by God. You have a place waiting for you in the riches of heaven. The secret to being overwhelmingly grateful is to recognize what you have.

Writing down a different blessing each day forces you to recognize all the many and diverse blessings God has given you. Instead of just being thankful, you will be thankful for your cat, Fluffy; for the sound of your children breathing as they sleep; and for God's amazing forgiveness, which washed away that terrible thing you said to your spouse.

As we see more clearly the many and diverse blessings that God showers upon us, we will be overwhelmed. We will join the Samaritan who fell at Jesus' feet and Zacchaeus, who gave away half of all he had, and Adam, who truly treasured his wife. We will be overwhelmingly grateful.

THE SECRET TO BEING OVERWHELMINGLY GRATEFUL IS TO RECOGNIZE YOU DON'T DESERVE ANY OF IT.

The crowds bustled in the temple courts. The sounds of bleating sheep and the smell of burning flesh filled the air. In the middle of the crowd, a Pharisee stood up. The Pharisees were highly respected by the people. They lived such outwardly holy lives. They were "better" than everyone else.

EVERYTHING WE HAVE AND EVERYTHING WE ARE IS A GIFT OF GOD'S GRACE.

The Pharisee lifted his arms to heaven and prayed in a loud voice for all to hear, "God, I thank you that I am better than everyone else. I fast twice a week even though you only command us to fast once a year. I give a tenth of all I have in my offerings, instead of just a tenth of what I *earn* like everyone else" (paraphrased from Luke chapter 18).

Meanwhile, another man, a tax collector like Zacchaeus, stood in a corner where no one could see him. He bowed his head and beat his breast. "God, have mercy on me, a sinner," he prayed with a heavy heart.

The Pharisee thought he could earn God's love. The tax collector recognized he didn't deserve to be forgiven. Of the two, Jesus tells us that the tax collector was the one who went home justified before God.

When I was a boy, McDonald's ran a series of commercials with a simple message: "You deserve a break today." Advertisers love to stroke our egos. "You deserve the best," they tell us. "You deserve a new car. You deserve a large-screen TV. You deserve our product."

We like to hear that. Just like the Pharisee in Jesus' story, we like to think we have earned what we have. We deserve it. In fact, we think we deserve much more. We work hard. We are good people. We deserve a break today.

Honestly, there is only one thing we deserve: God's punishment. The only thing we have earned with our lives is an eternity in hell. We are terrible sinners who do terrible things. If it were left to us, our homes, our lives, and our families would be in ruins.

Dr. Dwight L. Moody was a famous Christian preacher, writer, and professor from the 19th century. The story is told how one day Dr. Moody was returning from classes with a student. As they walked through the busy city streets of Chicago, they came upon a drunk passed out on the sidewalk in a pool of his own vomit. The student, trying to impress his professor, asked, "How could a person stoop so low?" Dr. Moody looked thoughtfully at his young student and said, "There, but for the grace of God, go I."

Like the tax collector in Jesus' story, Dr. Moody realized that everything good in his life was a gift of God's grace. If left up to him, Dr. Moody realized he could have been that drunk lying in a pool of his own vomit. The only reason he had become anything was by God's *grace*.

Grace. We hear that word all the time. What is grace? Grace is undeserved love. Grace is the mother of a murdered son hugging his murderer at the trial. Grace is the bullied child in school standing up for the boy who hurt him. Simply put, grace is loving the unlovable. Grace is God loving you.

Everything we have and everything we are is a gift of God's grace. The only thing we deserve from God is the fire of hell. Yet, he gives us house and home, friends and family, food and clothing, and everything we need for our body and life. Through Jesus, he forgives our dumb and dirty deeds. He gives us a home in heaven. We don't deserve any of it.

The secret to being overwhelmingly grateful is to recognize all that God has given us *and* to recognize that we don't deserve any of it.

CHAPTER 3
OVERWHELMING GENEROSITY

---

*"As we express our gratitude, we must
never forget that the highest appreciation
is not to utter words, but to live by them."*
— JOHN F. KENNEDY

A child stands with his mother in a packed elevator. The child sneezes. Someone nearby says, "Bless you."

Without hesitation, the mother looks down at her child and asks, "What do you say?"

Embarrassed, the child meekly looks up and says, "Thank you."

Is that what it means to be thankful?

Each year in the United States, millions of families gather in their homes on the fourth Thursday of November. We talk about being thankful. We eat turkey. We eat pie. We eat until we can't even move. Then we watch football.

Again I ask: Is that what it means to be thankful?

BEING THANKFUL IS AS MUCH ACTION AS IT IS ATTITUDE.

On the fourth Thursday of November each year, families on the island of Puerto Rico also gather together to celebrate. In Puerto Rico, Thanksgiving Day is called *El Día de Acción de Gracias*—literally "Thanks Action Day."

Now I think we're on to something.

Being thankful involves more than mere words. The Samaritan healed of his leprosy put his life on hold to thank Jesus. Zacchaeus showed his overwhelming gratitude with overwhelming generosity. Adam thanked God by treasuring and respecting his new companion. Being thankful is as much action as it is attitude.

AN EXAMPLE OF THANKS ACTION

It was the Tuesday of Holy Week. Two days earlier Jesus had ridden into Jerusalem surrounded by adoring fans singing, "Hosanna!" Three days later he would stand on the steps of the governor's palace as the unruly mob shouted, "Crucify him!"

For now, Jesus sat quietly on the steps of the temple courts, just outside the area of the temple known as the Court of Women. From there he watched as a steady line of people placed money into 13 trumpet-shaped boxes. They were giving their offerings to the Lord—their "thank yous" to God for sins forgiven, promises kept, and the everyday blessings of life.

Many well-dressed, prominent people walked by, some humbly giving their gifts of faith, others flaunting their offerings for all to see. Then a little old lady quietly passed by. She was a poor widow. No one seemed to notice as she placed two small coins in the coffers and continued on her way.

But Jesus noticed. He knew. He told the people, "I tell you the truth, this poor widow has put in more than all the others. All these people gave their gifts out of their wealth; but she out of her poverty put in all she had to live on" (Luke 21:3,4).

In our present-day world, we might wonder if that little old lady was suffering from dementia. How could she give away all she had? How would she eat? How would she survive? Why didn't somebody stop her?

The poor widow wasn't delusional. She was overwhelmingly grateful. In her poverty she recognized her great wealth. She truly understood that there is no such thing as a poor Christian.

She also trusted in God's promises. At the end of the Old Testament, God scolded his people for not giving their offerings. They were afraid that if they gave what they had to God, somehow they wouldn't have enough for themselves.

God, however, told them to test him—to give their offerings "and see if I will not throw open the floodgates of heaven and pour out so much blessing that you will not have room enough for it" (Malachi 3:10).

YOU CAN'T GIVE YOURSELF POOR.

God promises to bless a cheerful giver. The truth is that you cannot give yourself poor. Try it sometime. The more you give, the more God will bless you. The apostle Paul compared our giving to planting seeds. The more seeds you plant, the larger your harvest will be. "Whoever sows generously will also reap generously" (2 Corinthians 9:6).

Now don't get me wrong. This isn't like investing in the stock market. Don't think that if you put fifty dollars in the offering plate, you will get one hundred dollars in return the following week. God's blessings come in many forms. His best blessings don't have price tags—the gift of a grandchild, the peace of forgiveness, the joy of generosity.

That last one is important. Once you learn to let go, it's fun to give. There is joy in being overwhelmingly generous. Don't worry. You can't give yourself poor. The more you give, the richer you will be—and that will make you even more overwhelmingly thankful.

GIVE AS GOD HAS GIVEN TO YOU

Jesus once told the story of a multimillionaire who was going away on a long journey (Matthew 25:14-30). He left three of his servants in charge of his property. To each servant he gave according to the servant's ability. To the first he gave five talents. It is thought that a talent equals perhaps 75 pounds. In other words, the servant was given perhaps 375 pounds of gold or silver, a treasure worth millions of dollars today.

The second servant received two talents—still well over a million dollars. The third servant received one talent—less than the other two, but still worth hundreds of thousands of dollars today.

The first two servants used their millions. They invested them and made their money work for them. The third servant, however, went out, dug a hole, and hid his money in the ground.

When the multimillionaire returned, he called his servants to settle accounts. The first servant showed up. "Master," he said, "you entrusted me with five talents. See, I have gained five more."

"Well done, good and faithful servant!" the master replied. "You have been faithful with a few things; I will put you in charge of many things. Come and share your master's happiness!"

Next, the second servant came forward. "Master," he said, "you entrusted me with two talents; see, I have gained two more."

"Well done, good and faithful servant!" the master replied. "You have been faithful with a few things; I will put you in charge of many things. Come and share your master's happiness!"

Finally, the third servant came forward. He returned the money he had received, making excuses about why he hadn't used his talent to earn more. He said he was afraid of his master and didn't want to lose any of the money entrusted to him.

"You wicked, lazy servant!" the master replied. "You could have at least put the money in the bank and gained interest."

What is the point of Jesus' story? Just as the multimillionaire put each servant in charge of a different amount, so our God gives each of us varying gifts. God does not bless each person the same. To some he gives more material wealth; to others he gives less. To some he gives more gifts and abilities; to others he gives less. God in his grace blesses each person differently.

That being said, notice that even the servant who received only one talent still received a large amount. Even if God in his grace hasn't blessed you with as much material wealth as someone else, that does not mean you are poor. God has still blessed you richly. Remember, there is no such thing as a poor Christian!

The point of the parable is that God wants us to use what he has given us. He wants us to be faithful, to do our best with his blessings. God doesn't expect you to be the best. He expects you to do *your* best with what you have been given.

When the second servant came forward, the millionaire didn't ask him, "Why didn't you earn five like the first servant did?" No. He said, "Well done, good and faithful servant!" The second servant did his best with what he had been given.

GOD WANTS MORE THAN POLITE PLATITUDES.

In the same way today, God asks us to give as he has given to us. Consider your offerings in church as an example. One Sunday, two different women place $10 in the offering plate. The first woman earns $100 a week; the second, $1000 a week. Who gave more in the offering? Why was the widow's offering significantly more than the other offerings received at the temple? Because she gave all she had.

When it comes to your offerings, think in percentages, not in amounts. God doesn't want amounts. He wants your heart. He wants faithfulness. If he gives you more one week, then thank him by giving more to him in your offering. If he gives you less one week, then give him less. Give as God has given to you.

Remember also that God gives more than just material blessings. In fact, our English word *talent* is derived from this story in the Bible. God has given you different talents and abilities. So use those talents to God's glory. Give as he has given to you.

If he has given you the ability to teach, teach children of his grace. If he has given you the gift of music, use your melodies to echo your thanks. If he has given you the gift to cook, bake a cake for your elderly neighbor or prepare a pot roast for the struggling, single mom from your church.

In the end, be generous. Be generous as God has been generous with you. Be generous at church. Be generous with your children and grandchildren. Be generous with your neighbors and friends. Be generous with perfect strangers. Overwhelming gratitude leads to overwhelming generosity.

You are now ready to begin your *364 Days of Thanksgiving Journal*. As you write down one thing each day for which you are thankful, make sure to say "thank you" to God. Remember, you can't be thankful without having someone to thank.

Also remember that God wants more than polite platitudes. Overwhelming gratitude leads to overwhelming generosity. Make every day this year a "thanks action" day!

364 DAYS OF THANKSGIVING
JOURNAL

Before you begin your journey of thanksgiving, understand that this is a spiritual exercise. Have you ever set a goal to exercise physically every day? We start off with lofty goals, but too often we give up after only a few days.

Experts say it takes three to six weeks to form a good habit, so make this journal a consistent part of your daily routine. Set aside a specific time each day to think about and write down what you are thankful for. The best times for many are when they first wake up or when they go to bed at night. Do what works best for you.

To guide you as you keep your *364 Days of Thanksgiving Journal,* I have included passages from Scripture and personal reflections to help you recognize blessings in your life that you may have never noticed.

May God bless you richly as you discover how richly you are blessed!

The earth was exactly 144 hours old. In his amazing power and wisdom, God had caused all things to exist—the distant stars and the depths of the oceans, the largest whales and the tiniest bacteria. All of life that flows before us began in those six days.

And on the seventh day, God rested. But why did he rest? Was he tired? Was he worn out?

Our God doesn't get tired.

When God had finished his work of creation, he took a day to sit back and admire what he had done. He saw that it was good.

Then he commanded his Old Testament people to rest every seventh day, every Sabbath, so they too could sit back and admire what he had done for them.

That's what we do every time we worship at church. We take time away from our busy lives—time away from the noise and distractions of life—to sit quietly and admire what God in his love has done for us.

Are you having a hard time coming up with different things for which to thank God?

Take a Sabbath. Turn off your computer. Turn down the TV. Take a moment tonight to watch your children sleep, to stare at the stars, to walk through your house and see all the good things God has given you.

Then open up your Bible, sit back, and take a moment to admire what God has done for you.

I am thankfull for

DAY 1 Pajamas all day

DAY 2

DAY 3

DAY 4

DAY 5

DAY 6

DAY
7

DAY
8

DAY
9

DAY
10

DAY
11

DAY
12

DAY
13

_____
_____
_____
_____
_____
_____

DAY
14

_____
_____
_____
_____
_____

ADDITIONAL THOUGHTS

_____
_____
_____
_____
_____
_____
_____
_____
_____
_____
_____
_____
_____
_____

A few years ago, an elderly gentleman from our congregation passed away on a Sunday morning. I arrived at church that morning and found another member setting out Bibles for Sunday school.

In a somber voice, I told him, "Just so you know, Marvin passed away this morning."

Without looking up, the member happily responded, "Good for him!"

Suffice it to say, that wasn't the response I was expecting. It was, however, the correct response.

Usually we think of death and funerals as sad, somber occasions. A hole is left in our hearts when someone we love dies. We miss that person.

But Christian funerals are actually thanksgiving services. We can say "thank you" to God at a Christian funeral.

We can say "thank you" because Jesus died for that person. We can say "thank you" because the Holy Spirit gave that person faith. We can say "thank you" because he or she is enjoying the perfect paradise of heaven.

We can say "thank you" because our loved one no longer has to suffer the pains and problems of this world.

We can say "thank you" for the time God gave us with that person—for the blessings he gave us through that relationship.

Besides all that, Jesus won heaven for us as well. One day we will be reunited with our loved ones who died in Christ.

For that we can say "thank you" to God, even at a funeral.

IN HIS GREAT MERCY [GOD] HAS GIVEN US NEW BIRTH INTO A LIVING HOPE THROUGH THE RESURRECTION OF JESUS CHRIST FROM THE DEAD. — 1 PETER 1:3

DAY
15

DAY
16

DAY
17

DAY
18

DAY
19

DAY
20

DAY
21

DAY
22

DAY
23

DAY
24

DAY
25

DAY
26

DAY
27

DAY
28

ADDITIONAL THOUGHTS

In Romans 12:15, the apostle Paul encourages us to "rejoice with those who rejoice" and to "mourn with those who mourn."

Which is easier for you to do, rejoice with those who rejoice or mourn with those who mourn?

For most of us, it isn't difficult to mourn with those who mourn. When your friend's grandmother dies, you stand by her side at the funeral. When a hurricane or tornado strikes a community, people band together. In reality, it isn't hard for us to mourn with those who mourn.

But what about rejoicing with those who rejoice? Your best friend makes the cheerleading squad and you don't. Your next-door neighbor wins the lottery. Your sister ends up marrying a millionaire who looks like Brad Pitt.

It's not always easy to rejoice with those who rejoice. Why them? Why not me?

How can we be happy for other people's good fortunes? By recognizing how good God has been to us. When we remember how amazingly blessed and rich we are, we can say "thank you" to God for the good things he gives to others.

DAY
29

DAY
30

DAY
31

DAY
32

DAY
33

DAY
34

DAY
35

DAY
36

DAY
37

DAY
38

DAY
39

DAY
40

DAY
41

DAY
42

ADDITIONAL THOUGHTS

The story is told of a Christian man who lived in a two-story home. A terrible flood occurred in his town. As the water rose, he looked out a window on the first floor. A small boat with rescuers floated by.

"Hop in. We'll save you," they told him.

"No," the man said, "I trust in God. He will save me."

The waters continued to rise. The man took refuge on the second floor. He looked out a window. Another boat with rescuers floated by.

"Hop in. We'll save you."

"No, God will save me."

The waters continued to rise. The man now stood on the roof of his house. The water was up to his chin. Suddenly, a helicopter flew overhead. The occupants dropped a rope ladder down and shouted, "Climb up. We'll save you."

"No, God will save me."

The waters rose over the man's head, and he died. Because he was a Christian, however, he went to heaven.

When he arrived in heaven, he went straight to God.

"God, what happened? I trusted you to save me."

God smiled down at the man and said, "What more do you want? I sent you two boats and a helicopter."

So often we look for miracles and miss God at work in our daily lives.

MY GOD WILL MEET ALL YOUR NEEDS ACCORDING TO HIS GLORIOUS RICHES IN CHRIST JESUS. — PHILIPPIANS 4:19

DAY
43

DAY
44

DAY
45

DAY
46

DAY
47

DAY
48

DAY
49

DAY
50

DAY
51

DAY
52

DAY
53

DAY
54

DAY
55

DAY
56

ADDITIONAL THOUGHTS

The 1996 movie *Courage Under Fire* is the fictional story of Army Captain Karen Emma Walden, played by the actress Meg Ryan. In the movie, Captain Walden was the first woman to receive the Medal of Honor for valor in battle.

Though the movie is fiction, the reality of war it portrays rings true. Though Captain Walden never existed, true heroes like her fight for our freedom every day.

Our God has blessed many of us with the privilege of living in a great country. Americans enjoy freedoms of which many in the world can only dream.

But that freedom comes at a price. According to one Internet source, 1,326,612 soldiers in the history of the United States have given their lives in defense of freedom. Another 1,531,036 brave men and women have been wounded in battle.

That's nearly three million sons and daughters, husbands and wives, fathers and mothers.

Whenever I see a soldier on the street, I take my young daughter over to shake his or her hand and tell that soldier "thank you."

I will never be able to thank all the brave men and women who serve and sacrifice for me and my freedoms, but I can definitely thank God for them.

RESCUE ME AND DELIVER ME IN YOUR RIGHTEOUSNESS; TURN YOUR EAR TO ME AND SAVE ME. — PSALM 71:2

DAY
57

DAY
58

DAY
59

DAY
60

DAY
61

DAY
62

DAY
63

DAY
64

DAY
65

DAY
66

DAY
67

DAY
68

DAY
69

DAY
70

ADDITIONAL THOUGHTS

Soon after Charles Darwin published his book *The Origin of Species,* scientists began publishing lists of so-called vestigial organs. Simply put, a vestigial organ was a part of the human body that served no purpose. Supposedly, it was a leftover by-product of evolution. In 1890, lists of vestigial organs included up to 180 body parts that served no purpose—organs like the appendix and the tonsils.

Over the years, however, the list of vestigial organs has shrunk to zero as scientists have discovered that every part of the body serves a function. Every part of the body is important, even seemingly insignificant parts like nose hairs.

Though they are a nuisance at times, nose hairs filter the air we breathe and help us avoid getting sick.

Thank God for your nose hairs. Thank God for your pituitary gland and duodenum and pancreas. Thank God for your body.

May we always say with the psalmist, "I praise you [Lord,] because I am fearfully and wonderfully made" (Psalm 139:14).

DAY
71

DAY
72

DAY
73

DAY
74

DAY
75

DAY
76

DAY
77

DAY
78

DAY
79

DAY
80

DAY
81

DAY
82

DAY
83

_____
_____
_____
_____
_____
_____

DAY
84

_____
_____
_____
_____
_____

ADDITIONAL THOUGHTS

_____
_____
_____
_____
_____
_____
_____
_____
_____
_____
_____
_____
_____
_____

He was a cheat, a liar, and a murderer. The prophet pointed at him with the accusing finger of the Law. "You are the man!" the prophet told him.

"I have sinned against the LORD," the sinful king replied with head hung low.

"The LORD has taken away your sin," the prophet assured him with a heart happy to hear a repentant response (2 Samuel chapters 11 and 12).

He was a rebellious, ungrateful son. He did things that would make Las Vegas blush. He squandered everything he had. He fell on his knees before his heavenly Father. "I am no longer worthy to be called your son," he said with head hung low. The Father picked him up and hugged him as only a Father can (Luke 15:11-32).

He was a criminal who was getting what he deserved. In his dying breath, as the fires of hell nipped at his heels, he turned to his only hope. "Jesus, remember me when you come into your kingdom," he said with head hung low.

"I tell you the truth," his Savior assured him, "today you will be with me in paradise." And the doors to heaven swung wide open (Luke 23:39-43).

You are a cheat. You are a liar. You are a criminal and a murderer. You are a rebellious and ungrateful child.

And yet you are forgiven. Your sin has been completely washed away in Christ's blood. One day you will be with God in paradise where he will hug you as only a Father can.

Can we ever thank God enough for his forgiving love?

DAY
85

DAY
86

DAY
87

DAY
88

DAY
89

DAY
90

DAY
91

DAY
92

DAY
93

DAY
94

DAY
95

DAY
96

DAY
97

DAY
98

ADDITIONAL THOUGHTS

There are so many things for which I can thank God: my home, my children, the air I breathe and the food I eat, God's forgiveness and love and protection—oh, and also my brother's brain cancer.

What?! "Thank you, God, that my brother has brain cancer." How can I say such a thing? How can I thank God that my brother has a life-threatening illness?

How can you thank God that your marriage has challenges or that your son is flunking out of college? How can you thank God that your job is stressful or that your grandfather died?

That sounds crazy, but you can.

We can thank God for the problems and pains in our lives because we know they have a good purpose.

Read Jeremiah 29:11. Read Romans 8:28. Read the stories of Ruth and Job and Esther. God has a good purpose for everything that happens in the lives of his children. Even the pains and problems are blessings in disguise.

So, I will say it again: "Thank you, God, that my brother has brain cancer!"

WE . . . REJOICE IN OUR SUFFERINGS, BECAUSE WE KNOW THAT SUFFERING PRODUCES PERSEVERANCE; PERSEVERANCE, CHARACTER; AND CHARACTER, HOPE. AND HOPE DOES NOT DISAPPOINT US, BECAUSE GOD HAS POURED OUT HIS LOVE INTO OUR HEARTS BY THE HOLY SPIRIT, WHOM HE HAS GIVEN US. — ROMANS 5:3-5

DAY
99

DAY
100

DAY
101

DAY
102

DAY
103

DAY
104

DAY
105

DAY
106

DAY
107

DAY
108

DAY
109

DAY
110

DAY
111

DAY
112

ADDITIONAL THOUGHTS

In the movie *Cast Away,* Tom Hanks plays fictional FedEx employee Chuck Noland. After a plane crash, Noland finds himself stranded alone on a desert island in the South Pacific for over four years.

During his time on the island, a volleyball washes ashore. A bloody handprint on the ball soon becomes a face. Noland gives him the name Wilson.

Over the course of his four lonely years on the island, Wilson is Noland's only friend. Noland talks to him constantly. In the days before Noland is rescued, Wilson is swept out to sea. Noland mourns in tears the loss of his friend Wilson—an inanimate ball.

The poet John Donne once wrote, "No man is an island, entire of itself." In other words, God did not make us to be alone. Before creating Eve, God himself said, "It is not good for the man to be alone" (Genesis 2:18). We need other people.

Sometimes we don't necessarily care for the people around us. Sometimes we wish we could just be alone. But imagine being on a desert island for four years with no one to talk to but a volleyball!

Try to make a list of all the people God has placed in your life so that you are not alone. You may not have enough room on this page.

DAY
113

DAY
114

DAY
115

DAY
116

DAY
117

DAY
118

DAY
119

DAY
120

DAY
121

DAY
122

DAY
123

DAY
124

ADDITIONAL THOUGHTS

Have you heard of the Eucharist? *Eucharist* is a name some Christians use for the Sacrament of Holy Communion.

The name Eucharist comes from the Greek word for "thanksgiving." Holy Communion received that name because as Jesus celebrated the Passover with his disciples, he said a prayer of thanksgiving before giving them the bread and saying, "This is my body" (1 Corinthians 11:23,24).

Holy Communion is called the Eucharist, because as we receive it, we are saying "thank you" to God.

And well we should.

In the Sacrament of Holy Communion, our Savior gives us his body and blood as a covenant. It is a contract signed in blood, guaranteeing us the forgiveness of sins, life, and salvation. Every time we receive Holy Communion, we receive a reminder of what Jesus did for us in his great love.

Don't forget to thank God for his wonderful gift of Holy Communion.

DAY
127

DAY
128

DAY
129

DAY
130

DAY
131

DAY
132

DAY
133

DAY
134

DAY
135

DAY
136

DAY
137

DAY
138

ADDITIONAL THOUGHTS

Do you know what is the longest chapter of the Bible? The answer is Psalm 119. It has over 170 verses!

Psalm 119 is an *acrostic* poem. An acrostic poem is a poem in which the first line of every verse begins with a consecutive letter in the alphabet. The first letter of each verse of Psalm 119 coincides with the letters of the Hebrew alphabet.

Could you make an *acrostic* list of blessings in your life? In other words, could you come up with one personal blessing for every letter of the alphabet? Unless you play the xylophone, you may have a little trouble with a couple of the letters. But give it a try.

A _____   N _____

B _____   O _____

C _____   P _____

D _____   Q _____

E _____   R _____

F _____   S _____

G _____   T _____

H _____   U _____

I _____   V _____

J _____   W _____

K _____   X _____

L _____   Y _____

M _____   Z _____

DAY
141

DAY
142

DAY
143

DAY
144

DAY
145

DAY
146

DAY 147

DAY 148

DAY 149

DAY 150

DAY 151

DAY 152

ADDITIONAL THOUGHTS

Few people seem to be happy about their ages. When we are four years old, we want to be five. When we are in grade school, we want to be in junior high. When we are in junior high, we want to be in high school. When we are in high school, we want to be in college.

And when we are in college, we dream of the day we will finally graduate, the day we will get a job, the day we will get married and have kids. As young people, we are constantly looking and longing for tomorrow and next year.

Then as we get older, we become torn. We look back on our younger years and long for our glory days. At the same time, we look ahead and can't wait until retirement when we can finally take a break and do all the things we don't have time to do right now.

Then, when we finally retire, our bodies slow down and we wish we could go back to work and be as productive as we used to be.

Human nature never seems to be content with today. It always wants to look back with nostalgia on yesterday or to look ahead with yearning for tomorrow. The psalmist, however, reminds us to celebrate today. "This is the day the LORD has made," he wrote, "let us rejoice and be glad in it" (Psalm 118:24).

Every stage of life has its struggles, and every day has its blessings. Instead of constantly longing for a better day or a better age, look at the good God has given you today.

Yesterday is gone forever. Tomorrow may never come. God has given you the gift of today with the promise of forever in the joys of heaven. Be content with today.

DAY
155

DAY
156

DAY
157

DAY
158

DAY
159

DAY
160

DAY
161

DAY
162

DAY
163

DAY
164

DAY
165

DAY
166

DAY
167

DAY
168

ADDITIONAL THOUGHTS

"Teach us how to pray," Jesus' disciples once asked.

Jesus taught his disciples, "This, then, is how you should pray: *'Our Father in heaven, hallowed be your name, your kingdom come, your will be done on earth as it is in heaven. Give us today our daily bread. Forgive us our debts, as we also have forgiven our debtors. And lead us not into temptation, but deliver us from the evil one'* " (Matthew 6:9-13).

The Lord's Prayer has seven petitions—seven things for which we are asking God:

- Help us and others to keep your name holy.

- Come and reign as the King of our lives and hearts and in the hearts of others.

- Do what you think is best. We trust you.

- Give us what we need to live today.

- Forgive us our sins and help us to forgive others.

- Help us to avoid and to fight against temptations.

- Deliver us from anything that can do eternal harm to our souls.

You might have noticed that only one petition deals with our *physical,* material needs: "Give us today our daily bread." All the other petitions deal with our *spiritual* needs. When we pray, Jesus wants us to focus on what is most important—our spiritual needs.

When we thank God, how often do our thanks focus only on his physical blessings? Don't forget to thank God for his forgiveness and the faith he gives, for his Word and sacraments, for your church family, for the privilege to pray and praise him. Don't forget to thank God for spiritual blessings.

DAY
169

DAY
170

DAY
171

DAY
172

DAY
173

DAY
174

DAY
175

DAY
176

DAY
177

DAY
178

DAY
179

DAY
180

DAY
181

DAY
182

ADDITIONAL THOUGHTS

"Count your blessings." That phrase is used so often in our world today that it has become cliché. But do you know where that phrase comes from?

It comes from an old Jewish tradition. According to Jewish law, a faithful Jew will speak one hundred blessings every day. In other words, he or she will thank and praise God out loud for one hundred different things every single day.

So Orthodox Jews count their blessings every day to make sure they have said all one hundred. Imagine trying to come up with one hundred things every day for which to thank God. That must be hard to do.

Actually, it's not. As the prophet Jeremiah reminds us, God's mercies are new every morning (Lamentations 3:22,23).

You are now halfway through your yearlong journey of thanks. You now have nearly two hundred blessings for which you have thanked God. Take a moment to look over your list. Has it been hard to come up with a different blessing each day?

I'm guessing it hasn't. I imagine that some days you have a number of things you want to write down.

That is the fun of doing a spiritual exercise like this. It opens our eyes to the flood of blessings God showers on us every day. So keep it up. Keep counting your blessings!

DAY
183

DAY
184

DAY
185

DAY
186

DAY
187

DAY
188

DAY
189

DAY
190

DAY
191

DAY
192

DAY
193

DAY
194

ADDITIONAL THOUGHTS

The Constitution of the United States was ratified on September 17, 1787. The Bill of Rights was added in 1791. At that time, the United States Constitution was literally revolutionary. The First Amendment of the Bill of Rights states, "Congress shall make no law respecting an establishment of religion, or prohibiting the free exercise thereof; or abridging the freedom of speech, or of the press; or the right of the people peaceably to assemble, and to petition the government for a redress of grievances."

Americans are free to attend whatever churches we choose. We are free to speak our minds. The government cannot silence the press. We can get together, whenever we please, to disagree about the way our government is doing things.

Most of us, having lived our entire lives in the United States, often take such freedoms for granted. Few Americans know what it's like not to be able to worship, to speak, to gather without government interference.

Take the time one day this week to read through the Bill of Rights. What other freedoms do those who were born in this country enjoy?

Thank God for such freedoms.

I URGE, THEN, FIRST OF ALL, THAT REQUESTS, PRAYERS, INTERCESSION AND THANKSGIVING BE MADE FOR EVERYONE—FOR KINGS AND ALL THOSE IN AUTHORITY, THAT WE MAY LIVE PEACEFUL AND QUIET LIVES IN ALL GODLINESS AND HOLINESS. — 1 TIMOTHY 2:1,2

DAY
197

DAY
198

DAY
199

DAY
200

DAY
201

DAY
202

DAY
203

DAY
204

DAY
205

DAY
206

DAY
207

DAY
208

ADDITIONAL THOUGHTS

The story is told of two rival painters who were always trying to outdo each other. One day they decided to have a contest to see who was the better artist. The rule of the competition was simple: They would each create a painting that represented the idea of *peace*.

The first artist painted a beautiful mountain scene with a lake in the middle. The lake was as clear as a crystal and as blue as the sky. No wind or movement interrupted its tranquility. For the first artist, that was what peace looked like.

The second artist painted a strikingly different scene. He painted a violent waterfall. The sky was stormy, dark, and ominous. The wind blew across the canvas. Alongside the waterfall stood a gray, dead tree. A branch from the tree reached out in front of the waterfall. There, on that branch of the gray, dead tree in front of the violent waterfall in the middle of the storm, quietly sat a small bird, unaffected by the chaos that surrounded it. The bird was at peace.

On the night before he died, Jesus promised his disciples and us, "Peace I leave with you; my peace I give you. I do not give to you as the world gives. Do not let your hearts be troubled and do not be afraid" (John 14:27).

God promises to give us peace. But he doesn't promise to give us the peace of the first painting. He doesn't promise us a perfect paradise here on earth.

What he promises is to give us the peace of that little bird—peace in the middle of the storm. Knowing his love—knowing his promises of forgiveness, heaven, and his presence in our lives—gives us true peace.

Therefore, we can be at peace even as cancer ravages our bodies, even as our marriages struggle, even as violence fills the earth.

Thank you, God, for giving us peace the world cannot give.

DAY
211

DAY
212

DAY
213

DAY
214

DAY
215

DAY
216

DAY
217

DAY
218

DAY
219

DAY
220

DAY
221

DAY
222

ADDITIONAL THOUGHTS

There is a story told of a young pastor who arrived at a new church. Soon after moving in, he received a phone call from one of his new members. "My father is bedridden," she told him. "Would you come and visit him?"

"Sure," the young pastor agreed.

When he arrived at the house, the young woman met the pastor at the door. After some small talk, she directed him down the hall. "My father's room is the second door on the right," she said.

The pastor knocked on the door. Inside an elderly man lay on a bed. Facing the bed was a simple folding chair. "Hello," the pastor said.

"Hello," the man responded.

"I see you're expecting me," the pastor said.

"No. Who are you?" the elderly man asked.

"I'm your new pastor," the pastor replied. "I saw the chair and thought you were expecting me."

"Oh, the chair," the man replied. "Pastor, please have a seat." The man went on to explain how for years he had gone to church. He prayed in church and tried to pray at home, but he never really understood what prayer was.

"But then my friend told me to put a chair in front of me," the man said. "He told me to see Jesus sitting there, because Jesus is everywhere. Then he told me to talk to the chair as if I were talking to a friend—because that is what prayer is."

"I tried it," the man said, "and I liked it so much. I do it for at least an hour every day. But I have to be careful, because if my daughter catches me talking to an empty chair, she's going to send me to the old folks' home."

The pastor smiled and encouraged him to keep praying in that way.

Two weeks later, the pastor received a phone call. It was the daughter. She was in tears. Her father had died.

After talking a while, the daughter suddenly exclaimed, "By the way, pastor, something strange happened. It seems that in the moments right before he died, my father got up out of his bed, sat down on the floor, and laid his head on the chair next to his bed."

Thank you, God, for the gift of prayer.

THE LORD IS NEAR TO ALL WHO CALL ON HIM, TO ALL WHO CALL ON HIM IN TRUTH. — PSALM 145:18

DAY
225

DAY
226

DAY
227

DAY
228

DAY
229

DAY
230

DAY
231

DAY
232

DAY
233

DAY
234

DAY
235

DAY
236

DAY
237

DAY
238

ADDITIONAL THOUGHTS

One of my favorite words in the English language is the word *serendipity*. Do you know where that word comes from?

One cold winter's day in 1754, Horace Walpole, the earl of Orford, was reading a Persian fairy tale called *The Three Princes of Serendip*. The story touched him, and he wrote a letter to his friend Horace Mann to tell him of the thrilling approach to life he had discovered from the story.

According to the Oxford English Dictionary, the letter stated that the fairy tale told the story of three princes from the island of Sri Lanka, who "were always making discoveries, by accidents and sagacity, of things they were not in quest of." While looking for one thing, they found another.

Using the original name of the island, Serendip, Walpole coined the word *serendipity*. From that day on, Walpole's most significant and valuable experiences were those that happened to him when he least expected them.

Serendipity is a happy accident. Serendipity occurs when something beautiful breaks into the normal routine of our daily lives.

Serendipity occurred when the angel Gabriel appeared to Mary to tell her that she would be the mother of the Savior of the world (Luke 1:26-38). Serendipity occurred when Jesus appeared to Saul on the road to Damascus (Acts 9:1-19). Serendipity occurs when you find a $20 bill lying in the parking lot, when your unromantic husband suddenly surprises you with flowers, when you are shopping for clothes for your kids and suddenly find the boots you've always wanted *on sale*.

Our God is serendipitous. Every so often he sends a happy little accident, a pleasant surprise, to break the monotony of our everyday lives. Don't forget to thank God for those wonderful, little serendipitous surprises.

DAY
239

DAY
240

DAY
241

DAY
242

DAY
243

DAY
244

DAY
245

DAY
246

DAY
247

DAY
248

DAY
249

DAY
250

ADDITIONAL THOUGHTS

I was baptized on September 1, 1973, when I was just four days old. When were you baptized? I would imagine that some of you were baptized as infants, others as teenagers, others as adults.

If you are a Christian, though, most likely you were at some point baptized. Actually, as Christians we usually don't say that we *were* baptized.

We say, "We *are* baptized."

The word *baptize* comes from a Greek word that simply means "to wash." In Baptism God doesn't wash dirt off our bodies but, rather, sin from our souls (1 Peter 3:21).

Through water and the promises of his Word, the Holy Spirit gives and strengthens faith (Acts 2:38). Through faith we receive the forgiveness and heaven that Jesus won for us on the cross.

Baptism isn't just something that happened to you in the past. The promises of Baptism are lifelong promises. The benefits of Baptism are ongoing.

You *are* baptized. Through the faith given and strengthened in Baptism you live in a constant state of forgiveness, washed of your sins in Jesus' blood.

Thank God that you *are* baptized.

DAY
253

DAY
254

DAY
255

DAY
256

DAY
257

DAY
258

DAY
259

DAY
260

DAY
261

DAY
262

DAY
263

DAY
264

ADDITIONAL THOUGHTS

I recently did the calculations. If my math is correct, there is a prayer I have said at least 39,420 times in my life. As soon as I learned to speak, my parents taught me to pray at every meal: *Oh, give thanks to the Lord, for he is good; his mercy endures forever. Amen* (based on Psalm 107:1).

Do you say that prayer at mealtime? It's a prayer found throughout the book of Psalms.

It's a prayer God's people would say as they approached the city of Jerusalem for high festivals. It's a prayer they would say as they offered their sacrifices in the temple. It's a prayer they would say as they remembered God's grace in the Passover.

It's a prayer I have spoken at least 39,420 times to thank God for the food he provides.

Honestly, though, those words don't just apply to the food I eat. God shows his goodness in every aspect of my life. I should be saying that prayer all day long.

I have a wonderful wife. *Oh, give thanks to the Lord, for he is good.* I have healthy children. *Oh, give thanks to the Lord, for he is good.* I have a home, clothes, air conditioning, and an iPhone. *Oh, give thanks to the Lord, for he is good.*

His mercy endures forever. You are forgiven for every one of your sins because of Jesus. You will live forever in the glories of heaven where you will say this prayer over and over again for eternity.

So pray it now here on earth. Pray it at mealtime. But also pray it as you see and recognize God's goodness and mercy in every aspect of your life. Oh, give thanks to the Lord!

DAY
267

DAY
268

DAY
269

DAY
270

DAY
271

DAY
272

DAY
273

DAY
274

DAY
275

DAY
276

DAY
277

DAY
278

ADDITIONAL THOUGHTS

Do you know who Thomas Crapper is? His name says it all. Though he did not invent the flush toilet, he is credited with popularizing it and making it accessible to the common person.

According to many experts, the toilet has saved more lives in the last two hundred years than any other single invention.

Two hundred years ago, people would often dump their bodily waste into the street. Cities stank. Disease was rampant. But the flushable toilet changed all that.

Much has changed in two hundred years.

Two hundred years ago, there were no computers or cell phones. In fact, there were no telephones. Two hundred years ago, there were no cars or airplanes. There were no electronic appliances. The light bulb hadn't even been invented yet.

One of the greatest gifts God has given to people is the ability to create—to invent. Through that creative gift, God has given us many of the present-day comforts we take for granted.

Take some time this week to walk through your house and garage. Make a list of all the present-day marvels you own that didn't exist two hundred years ago.

Then thank God for creating us to be creative.

I PRAISE YOU BECAUSE I AM FEARFULLY AND WONDERFULLY MADE.
— PSALM 139:14

DAY
281

DAY
282

DAY
283

DAY
284

DAY
285

DAY
286

DAY
287

DAY
288

DAY
289

DAY
290

DAY
291

DAY
292

ADDITIONAL THOUGHTS

In the olden days, before refrigerators, people used what were called icehouses to preserve their food. An icehouse had thick walls, no windows, and a tightly fitted door. In the winter when streams and lakes were frozen over, large blocks of ice were cut out and transported to the icehouses where they were covered with sawdust. Often the ice would last well into the summer.

The story is told of a man who lost a valuable watch while working in an icehouse. He searched long and hard for it, but could not find it. His fellow workers helped him carefully dig through the wet sawdust looking for the watch, but to no avail.

Later, while everyone else was out to lunch, a small boy who had heard about the lost watch slipped into the icehouse. A few minutes later he emerged with the watch.

Amazed, the men asked him how he found it. "I closed the door," the boy replied, "I laid down in the sawdust and kept very quiet. Soon I heard the watch ticking."

We live in a stereo, surround sound world. With all that noise, it's hard to hear. It's hard to hear God's voice speaking to us.

God doesn't usually yell. He doesn't usually communicate in thunderbolts or in burning bushes. No. God speaks to us in the gentle whisper of his Word. He speaks to us as we sit quietly in church hearing his Word read to us. He whispers into our ears as we sit quietly in our homes reading our Bibles.

Often the question is not whether God is speaking to us but whether we are taking the time to sit quietly and listen. So turn off the TV, silence your iPhone, and put your child's video game away. Sit together as a family, listening to God speak to you through his Word.

Through the gentle whisper of his Word, God will convict you and comfort you. Through the gentle whisper of his Word, he will teach you and guide you and give you hope.

Take the time to listen to God gently whisper to you through his Word and then whisper back a gentle and heartfelt "thank you."

MY SHEEP LISTEN TO MY VOICE; I KNOW THEM, AND THEY FOLLOW ME. I GIVE THEM ETERNAL LIFE, AND THEY SHALL NEVER PERISH; NO ONE CAN SNATCH THEM OUT OF MY HAND. — JOHN 10:27,28

DAY
295

DAY
296

DAY
297

DAY
298

DAY
299

DAY
300

DAY
301

DAY
302

DAY
303

DAY
304

DAY
305

DAY
306

DAY
307

DAY
308

ADDITIONAL THOUGHTS

"Give us today our daily bread."

We say those words every time we pray the Lord's Prayer, but for what are we asking when we pray, "Give us today our daily bread" (Matthew 6:11)? Are we asking that God give us a loaf of bread every day?

In Jesus' day, people didn't have the selection of food we have today. They didn't have grocery stores filled with 20 different kinds of bread and 75 different brands of cereal. They didn't have McDonald's and Subway and Burger King on every corner.

The one food they ate every day—the one food they needed to survive—was bread. If they didn't have bread, they starved.

When we pray, "Give us today our daily bread," we are asking God to provide for our physical needs. We are asking for food, clothing, and shelter. We are asking for what we need to live today.

You'll notice, however, Jesus didn't say, "Give us tomorrow our daily bread." Don't get me wrong. To faithfully use God's gifts, it's good for us to plan for tomorrow and next year and ten years from now.

But God doesn't want us to worry about tomorrow. He doesn't want us living for next year. He wants us living for him today. He wants us to focus on each day—to live in the present and trust that he is in control of the future.

So go ahead and invest in your 401K, buy your life insurance policy, and plan for the future. That is a responsible use of God's gifts. Meanwhile, however, don't *worry* about the future.

Instead, pray every day, "Give us today our daily bread." Then thank God every day for the bread he provides.

DAY
309

DAY
310

DAY
311

DAY
312

DAY
313

DAY
314

DAY
315

DAY
316

DAY
317

DAY
318

DAY
319

DAY
320

DAY
321

DAY
322

ADDITIONAL THOUGHTS

When I was a senior in high school, my class took a trip to Washington D.C. We visited most of the tourist sites. We toured the Smithsonian, the Capitol, and the White House, and we stopped at most of the monuments.

Two stops, however, affected me more than the others: the Tomb of the Unknown Soldier and the Vietnam Memorial.

I saw the changing of the guard at the Tomb of the Unknown Soldier. I read the names on the Vietnam Memorial. As I did, I came to realize for the first time in my young life the profound sacrifices men and women have made to protect me and my freedom.

I have what I have today because of the sacrifices of others.

The same can be said spiritually. The church father Tertullian was right when he said, "The blood of the martyrs is the seed of the church." Throughout the centuries, men and women gave their lives so the good news of God's Word could reach us today.

Thousands upon thousands of believers have died throughout history so that future generations can know their Savior. They have left for us an example. They have left for us a legacy.

Even today God has placed in each of our lives men and women who have sacrificed so that we could know Jesus—those who have lived and shared their faith with us and others.

I am a Christian today because of the faith of my father and mother, my grandparents and great-grandparents. I am a pastor because of their example and the encouragement of countless other Christians.

Who in your life has impacted and encouraged your faith?

REMEMBER YOUR LEADERS, WHO SPOKE THE WORD OF GOD TO YOU. CONSIDER THE OUTCOME OF THEIR WAY OF LIFE AND IMITATE THEIR FAITH. — HEBREWS 13:7

DAY
323

DAY
324

DAY
325

DAY
326

DAY
327

DAY
328

DAY
329

DAY
330

DAY
331

DAY
332

DAY
333

DAY
334

ADDITIONAL THOUGHTS

In 1990, country singer Garth Brooks released a song that raced to the top of the charts. It was called "Unanswered Prayers."

The song tells the story of how he and his wife attended a football game at his old high school. There he ran into his old high school flame.

As he and his ex-girlfriend spoke, Brooks thought back to high school and how every night he had prayed to God that he and this girl would be together forever. But then Brooks turned and looked at his wife and thought, "Sometimes I thank God for unanswered prayers."

The truth is that Garth Brooks only got it half right. There are actually no unanswered prayers. God did answer Garth Brooks' prayer.

He said "no."

God sometimes says "no" to our prayers. He says "no" because what we ask for is not always what is best for us. He says "no" because he has something better for us.

When God gives us what we ask for in our prayers, it's easy to say "thank you." But have you ever thanked God for saying "no"?

"I KNOW THE PLANS I HAVE FOR YOU," DECLARES THE LORD, "PLANS TO PROSPER YOU AND NOT TO HARM YOU, PLANS TO GIVE YOU HOPE AND A FUTURE." — JEREMIAH 29:11

DAY
337

DAY
338

DAY
339

DAY
340

DAY
341

DAY
342

DAY
343

DAY
344

DAY
345

DAY
346

DAY
347

DAY
348

ADDITIONAL THOUGHTS

"What is heaven like, Daddy?" How many of us have tried to answer that in terms a four-year-old could understand?

In 2010, Todd Burpo, a Methodist pastor from Nebraska, released a book called *Heaven Is for Real*. The book documents the story of Burpo's four-year-old son, Colton, who says that he went to heaven while undergoing an emergency appendectomy. Colton describes in great detail the heaven he saw.

After reading the book, many of us find ourselves asking, "Did he really see heaven?"

What is heaven like? We all want to know. But God doesn't tell us . . . exactly.

In the Bible, God describes the beauty and joy of heaven in a number of ways: a crystal sea, Jerusalem the golden, paradise regained. The pictures of heaven in the Bible, however, are just that: word pictures, symbols, figures. God is describing in human terms what human minds cannot fully comprehend. Human words cannot fully describe the wonders of heaven. Human minds cannot begin to fathom it.

What we can say for sure about heaven is that God will be there, together with all our loved ones who died in Christ. We can also say what won't be there—no more sin or sadness, no more sickness or death (Revelation 21:4).

The way I usually try to help people understand what heaven will be like is by asking them to imagine a really fun day. You know, a family get-together, a day at the beach, a day so full of fun that you end it with the words, "What a great day!"

Now multiply that feeling by a thousand and imagine it never ending. That is just a small glimpse of what heaven will be like.

Thank you, Jesus, for the happiness of heaven that is waiting for me.

DAY
351

DAY
352

DAY
353

DAY
354

DAY
355

DAY
356

DAY
357

DAY
358

DAY
359

DAY
360

DAY
361

DAY
362

363

364

ADDITIONAL THOUGHTS

Well, you've made it. A year has passed since you began this journey of thanksgiving. I hope and pray that this book and this journey have helped you see God's goodness and grace in your life.

On day 365, I encourage you to read through your entire *364 Days of Thanksgiving Journal*. See what God did for you this last year. See his hand working in your life. See his grace.

Now doesn't it make you wonder how many more days you could have gone on, listing God's blessings without repeating? When would you run out of things for which to thank God? Try it. Start another year of thanksgiving. Live another year of thanks action.

May your life be filled with overwhelming thanks to the Giver of all good things!

ADDITIONAL THOUGHTS

ADDITIONAL THOUGHTS

ADDITIONAL THOUGHTS

ADDITIONAL THOUGHTS

ADDITIONAL THOUGHTS

ADDITIONAL THOUGHTS

ADDITIONAL THOUGHTS

ADDITIONAL THOUGHTS

ADDITIONAL THOUGHTS

ADDITIONAL THOUGHTS

ADDITIONAL THOUGHTS

ADDITIONAL THOUGHTS

ADDITIONAL THOUGHTS

ADDITIONAL THOUGHTS

ADDITIONAL THOUGHTS

ADDITIONAL THOUGHTS

ADDITIONAL THOUGHTS

ADDITIONAL THOUGHTS

ADDITIONAL THOUGHTS

ADDITIONAL THOUGHTS